ENGLISH
À LA CARTOON

Edited by
Albert H. Small, Ph.D.

PASSPORT BOOKS
NTC/Contemporary Publishing Company

Dedicated to
Sheila
Who Knows That
Education and Entertainment
Can Go Hand in Hand

Also available:
French à la Cartoon
German à la Cartoon
Spanish à la Cartoon

Published by Passport Books
An imprint of NTC/Contemporary Publishing Company
4255 West Touhy Avenue, Lincolnwood (Chicago), Illinois 60646-1975 U.S.A.
Copyright © 1993 by NTC/Contemporary Publishing Company
All rights reserved. No part of this book may be reproduced, stored in a retrieval system, or transmitted in any form or by any means, electronic, mechanical, photocopying, recording, or otherwise, without the prior permission of NTC/Contemporary Publishing Company.
Printed in the United States of America
International Standard Book Number: 0-8442-0683-0

7 8 9 0 VP 9 8 7 6 5 4

Contents

A—Careful!—
Word in Advance

English is probably the world's most important language—not just because of the number of people who speak it, but because of its significance in international trade and in international social, cultural, and political relations.

The language of England was carried by English ships and English settlers to North America, to parts of Africa, to Asia, and to Australia. When the settlers in eastern America rebelled against the English king, they formed the United States, which eventually reached across the continent from the Atlantic to the Pacific and beyond to Alaska and Hawaii. English settlers were the largest group to arrive in Canada, although French remains the primary language in the province of Quebec. In the Eastern Hemisphere, English is a major language in Australia, as well as in India, Pakistan, South Africa, and Egypt—to name some of the largest countries.

Indeed, English as a second language helps bind together some countries, such as India and the Philippines, where there are many local languages that are not understood throughout the country.

English may be said to have been built from two sources: the Anglo-Saxon language of the inhabitants of England, before the eleventh century, and the French and Latin words and phrases brought by William the Conqueror after the year 1066.

One of the interesting features of the English language is how we can use the same words for different meanings. Take, for example, the common but useful verb *go*.

You can *go along* a corridor looking for somebody's room, but you can *go along* with (accept) the decision of the majority, even if you voted against it. You can *go down* the stairs into the basement, but your team can *go down* in defeat in a football game. You can *go into* a room, but a committee can *go into* the question of spending money for something. You can *go with* a friend to the movies, but you should know that a pink plaid shirt does not *go with* purple and green striped trousers.

And while *go* typically means "moving from one place to another" (for example, go home, go to school, go to work), it sometimes does not have that meaning. "I'm *going* to sit still" uses *go* to mean the future (instead of "I *will* sit still").

Comedians and cartoonists love these multiple meanings. They can say the doctor charges ten dollars to *look down* your throat, but fifteen dollars to *look up* your birth certificate. They can also make fun of popular expressions that do not quite mean what they seem to. Said one comedian: "My neighbor has a circular driveway . . . he can't get out!" (Of course, a circular driveway is actually semicircular.)

Although English is a single language, major and minor differences exist in the way it is used in different places: In the North of the United States, you can *carry* a package to school; but in the South, you can *carry* a child to school—not in your arms, but by walking hand in hand with him or her. In New York City you stand *on line* as you wait to get into a theater, but elsewhere in the country, you stand *in line*.

Between the United States and England, the differences are greater. If you say, "Last night I got a flat," in England it probably means that you were able to rent an apartment. However, in the United States, the same sentence would mean that your automobile had a punctured tire.

Different words and expressions were added as English traveled around the world. In India, because laborers often had to "go down" into the cellar to store goods, *godown* became the word for warehouse. If a young, single Indian man is seeking a bride who likes to take care of the home, he may advertise in a newspaper for a "homely girl"— but elsewhere, *homely* means "not very pretty."

Spoken English can be even more confusing. A New Yorker can compress three words into one syllable when he asks a friend at lunchtime, "Jeat?" ("Did you eat?") To that the friend might answer, "No, djou?" ("No, did you?")

English frightens people who are studying it because its spelling is not simple and obvious the way it is, for example, in Spanish. But letters and sounds do relate to one another—it simply requires learning the different sounds of the various groups of letters.

Now that you have read how complicated English can be, why should a book of cartoon humor improve your reading skills?

First, somebody once said that a picture is worth a thousand words. If that picture happens to be funny—a wife lighting a firecracker in her husband's ear or the Board of Directors throwing pies at one another during a meeting—you will want to read the words that explain the joke. And there is nothing so easy to remember as a good joke.

Second, cartoon humor uses the words we all use to talk to one another. So you will be learning the words that are important to read in everyday life—in newspapers, magazines, instruction books, and the like. And, for an amusing challenge, be sure not to miss the "An Extra Smile" section at the bottom of each cartoon page.

Finally, humor makes learning enjoyable. Any type of learning always makes the mind work. If the job can be made easier because you smile as you learn, so much the better!

A Technical Comment—or Two

Improving your reading skills can be fun—especially when it helps you to read newspapers, magazines, and other things you enjoy. But let's face it—reading can also become complicated. In this book we're going to try to keep as much of the fun as we can, and burden you with a minimum of complications.

In most languages, and especially in English, words can have many meanings. Under each cartoon, and in the glossary, we almost always limit ourselves to the meaning in the cartoon and the words following it. So don't be surprised if you come across other meanings in your reading. Once in a while we will point out how different meanings or how an expression reflects culture in the United States. You can find these explanations in the **Points of Interest** section at the back of the book.

To help you learn to read well, we have included four special sections. **The Pronouns** are substitutes for names and nouns and do other useful things in sentences. There are **Three Important Verbs** in English that are heavily used in most writing. Next, some popular **Contractions** are given. We often use contractions to make words and sentences shorter. Then we have a list of the **Little Words**— like and, but, and if—that hold sentences together. These are shown in four languages—English, Spanish, French, and German. If you learned another language before English, this list may be very helpful.

The Pronouns

This is not an exhaustive list of pronouns in English. Rather, it is an illustration of how common pronouns you will encounter in the cartoon captions can be used in conversation.

Personal Pronouns

Subject Pronouns

I	**we**
you	
he, she, it	**they**

Object Pronouns

me	**us**
you	
him, her, it	**them**

Examples:

I laugh at cartoons.

Gertrude married **him**.

Possessive Pronouns

With another word

my	**our**
your	
his, her,	**their**
its	

Without another word

mine	**ours**
yours	
his, hers,	**theirs**
its	

Examples:

Our house is purple.

The purple house is **ours**.

Demonstrative Pronouns

this	**these**
that	**those**

Example:

This is my favorite joke.

Those were not funny jokes.

Interrogative Pronouns

who	**which**
whom	**whose**
what	

Examples:

What happened to the cat?
Who is driving the car?

Indefinite Pronouns

Singular			Plural	S. or P.
anybody	**everybody**	**no one**	**both**	**all**
anyone	**everyone**	**nothing**	**few**	**any**
anything	**neither**	**one**	**many**	**none**
each	**nobody**	**someone**	**several**	**some**

Examples

Everybody loves to smile.   **No one** likes to frown.
Many read the Sunday comics.
Some of the pie is gone.   **Some** of the comics are clever.

Three Important Verbs

to be	to have	to go

Present

I am	I have	I go, am going
you are	you have	you go, are going
he, she, it is	he, she, it has	he, she, it goes, is going
we are	we have	we go, are going
they are	they have	they go, are going

Past

I was	I had	I went
you were	you had	you went
he, she, it was	he, she, it had	he, she, it went
we were	we had	we went
they were	they had	they went

Future

I will be	I will have	I will go
you will be	you will have	you will go
he, she, it will be	he, she, it will have	he, she, it will go
we will be	we will have	we will go
they will be	they will have	they will go

Contractions

In order to make characters sound like people do in real-life conversations, many cartoonists use contractions with pronouns and verbs in their captions. Below are some of the most common contractions.

not		**be**	
cannot	can't	I am	I'm
is not	isn't	you are	you're
will not	won't	he, she, it is	he's, she's, it's
should not	shouldn't	we are	we're
would not	wouldn't	they are	they're

have		**will**	
I have	I've	I will	I'll
you have	you've	you will	you'll
he, she, it has	he's, she's, it's	he, she, it will	he'll, she'll, it'll
we have	we've	we will	we'll
they have	they've	they will	they'll

Examples:

I've told them not to go.	**I have** told them not to go.
He'd do it again if he could.	**He would** do it again if he could.
She'll call you later.	**She will** call you later.
What's your problem?	**What is** your problem?

NOTE: The handy little apostrophe (') also appears in cartoon captions—and in written dialogues—to show that one or more letters are missing from a word.

Am I **supposed** to laugh now?	Am I **s'posed** to laugh now?
He's **just** teasing you.	He's **jus'** teasing you.
She's **thinking about them.**	She's **thinkin' 'bout 'em.**

Little Words

English	Spanish	French	German
a, an	un, una, uno	un, une	ein, einen
after	después	après	nach
again	otra vez	encore	wieder
and	y	et	und
because	porque	parce que	weil
before	antes	avant	vorher
but	pero	mais	aber
each	cada	chaque	jede
for	para	pour	für
here	aquí	ici	hier
if	si	si	wenn
in	en	dans, en	im
less	menos	moins	weniger
more	más	plus	mehr
never	nunca	ne. . .jamais	nie
no	no	non	nein
nothing	nada	ne. . .rien	nichts
now	ahora	maintenant	jetze
of	de	de	von
on	puesto	sur	auf
only	solo	seulement	nur
over	superior	sur	über
perhaps	acaso	peut-être	vielleicht
please	por favor	s'il vous plaît	bitte
still	todavía	encore	noch
the	el, la, los, las	le, la, les	der, die, das
then	entonces	puis	denn
there	allí	là, y	da
to	a, al, para	à	zu
under	inferior	sous, dessous	unter
when	cuándo	quand	wann
why?	¿por qué?	pourquoi?	weshalb?
yes	sí	oui	ja

Introducing . . . the Artists!

Aaron Bacall never took an art lesson; on the contrary, he has graduate degrees in organic chemistry and management. Maybe the secret of his success as a cartoonist is that he was born in Brooklyn when the famous Dodgers were still playing baseball at Ebbets Field. Today he still has a New York City address, but across the Verrazzano Bridge from Brooklyn, in Staten Island.

As a schoolboy he drew cartoons on brown paper bags and stuffed them in the pockets of his yellow jeans, which he wore with a yellow shirt. He says he looked like an ear of corn and thinks that is why he began adding "corny" captions to his drawings. Now his cartoons are used by advertising agencies, book publishers, and magazine editors in this country and abroad, ranging from the *Wall Street Journal* to *Punch* magazine in England.

Where does a cartoonist's sense of humor come from? Aaron Bacall thinks it's a way of looking at the world. Bacall says you need "an antenna always aimed at the ridiculous." That's the way the world looks if you tilt your head and look at just the right angle, says Bacall. Then you need the ability to condense the humor into a few perceptive lines.

"Karlos Barney" is not one but two cartoonists: Karl Nilsson and Barney Judge, both from the Detroit area. They claim to share two things: a fear of toasters and an ability to find bizarre irony in everyday life. "When we first started," says Barney Judge, "we thought we'd set the world on fire. Now we'd be happy to just set a few kitchen tables on fire." Karl Nilsson adds: "Cartooning is in our blood. But with the help of modern antibiotics, we're able to lead normal lives."

Barney Judge attended the University of Michigan, then majored in graphic communications at Detroit's Center for Creative Studies. His editorial illustrations often appear in major newspapers, and in 1986 he won the New York Art Directors' Award for his outstanding newspaper art. Clients for his freelance studio include Northwest Airlines and the *Detroit News*.

Karl Nilsson majored in art history and philosophy at Wayne State University. Currently he owns Nilsson Advertising, and he writes a weekly humor column called "Fear and Loafing in Suburbia," which appears in over a dozen newspapers.

The team describes how they get to work. "First we assume one of three standard comedy positions," says Nilsson, "then Barney holds the pencil and I push the paper around." Judge adds, "If either of us doesn't think a panel is funny we reject it—unless I whine a lot."

Barney Judge says, "We started out with the motto 'Two morons for the price of one,' but that sounded too boastful." Karl Nilsson claims, "Now our business card reads 'Two Pseudo-Intellectuals—No Waiting'."

Randy Glasbergen—who draws "The Better Half" under the pen name **"Jay Harris,"** is one of the most widely and frequently published American cartoonists. In addition to the more than 12,000 Glasbergen cartoons published in *Good Housekeeping*, the *Wall Street Journal, New Woman, Cosmopolitan*, the *National Enquirer, McCall's, Women's World, First*, and other periodicals in 25 countries, his work is often used in advertising, calendars, books, greeting cards, trade magazines, and religious publications.

Formerly a member of the Humor Writing staff at Hallmark Cards in Kansas City, Missouri, Glasbergen is now freelancing. Hallmark, Gibson Greetings, Paramount Cards, Oatmeal Studios, and other North American greeting-card publishers are among his clients.

He has been creating the widely syndicated "Better Half" cartoon panels since 1982.

Born in 1957, Randy Glasbergen presently lives in a small town in rural upstate New York with his wife and four children.

When **John Louthan** draws cartoons about the business world, his work is based on his experience. Although a native of Oklahoma, John took a degree in Arts and Letters at the Portland (Oregon) State University. After graduation he took a job there as an advertising representative. From this he shifted to a career as a stockbroker, interrupting this to become owner and operator of retail stores specializing in unfinished furniture.

But the follies and frustrations of the business world found such expression in John Louthan's humor that he turned to freelance cartooning and writing comedy material for leading entertainers. His material has been used by Phyllis Diller, *The Tonight Show*, Merv Griffin, and Las Vegas entertainers. His cartoons have been published in *The Saturday Evening Post, Chicago* magazine, *Writer's Digest*, and *Sales and Marketing Management*. As his syndicated "Briefcase" cartoons show, financiers, lawyers, doctors, personnel directors, and others who try to convince the world of their importance are targets for John Louthan's humorous pen.

In his spare time, he restored an 80-year-old home in which he lives with his wife, an occupational therapist, and his two daughters.

Jerry Marcus sold his first cartoon for $2.50 to a paper published for schoolchildren by a local bank. At the time he was still a student at Public School 165 in Brooklyn.

His career took off in earnest after he finished his studies at the Cartoonists and Illustrators School. His distinctive work began appearing in more and more national magazines—including *The New Yorker, Look, The Saturday Evening Post, McCall's*, and *Ladies Home Journal*—as well as foreign magazines such as *Paris Match*. His "Trudy" cartoon panels are distributed by King Features to more than 150 newspapers.

Despite an innate talent for finding the ludicrous in everyday situations, he works hard at cartooning. He has been known to spend as many as 20 hours a day at the drawing board in his Ridgefield, Connecticut, studio. Even when relaxing in an easy chair, he may be thinking up jokes for his cartoons. "Believe it or not," he says, "there have been times when I've dreamed of a gag and drawn it when I woke up." That's why he keeps a piece of drawing paper handy by his bed.

Even though his cartoons have received international acclaim, Jerry may prefer to tell you about the time he played the role of a British solider in the Otto Preminger film *Exodus.* He is a longtime movie buff (his expert knowledge goes back to the silent films). In addition to studying the stars of Hollywood, he studies the stars of the sky, as an enthusiastic amateur astronomer.

Henry Martin has been amusing the sophisticated readers of *The New Yorker* magazine for more than 38 years. But, as the examples of his "Good News/Bad News" cartoons in this book show, his humor can be simple and obvious.

In addition to *The New Yorker*, Martin's cartoons have appeared in many magazines, including *The Saturday Evening Post, Look, Ladies' Home Journal, Good Housekeeping, The Saturday Review, Gourmet, TV Guide, Changing Times*, and *Punch,* England's popular humor magazine.

His cartoons have been collected in three books: *Good News/Bad News, Yak Yak! Blah! Blah!,* and *All Those in Favor.* He has also illustrated books and designed book jackets, as well as greeting cards and games. The Pavilion of Humor in Montreal was but one of a number of shows at which his cartoons have been shown.

The *Boston Globe,* commenting on the book *Good News/Bad News,* said, "Henry Martin is funny, funny, mostly about the idiocies of making a living." You may open your daily newspaper to see one of his "Good News/Bad News" cartoons, which are syndicated by Tribune Media Services.

Henry Martin is a Princeton graduate and also attended the American Academy of Art in Chicago. He makes his home in Princeton, New Jersey, with his wife, their two daughters, and two cats.

Ted Martin—Animals have been cartoon favorites since even before Mickey Mouse became a worldwide celebrity. Snoopy in the "Peanuts" cartoons and Garfield the cat are among current favorites. But one of the most outrageous is Ted Martin's "Pavlov."

Ted Martin says his parents were wandering minstrels in England though neither played an instrument. Similarly, "Pavlov's" parent—Ted Martin—improvises. His wry wit and pen are expressed in right-handed drawings, although Martin is left-handed. Educated in England, where he attended art school, Martin moved to Canada in 1962, and now he runs an art studio in Toronto.

His cartoons have appeared in *Paris Match, Gourmet* magazine, *Evergreen Review, McLean's* magazine, and *TV Guide.* He has produced a daily cartoon for the *Toronto Sun* since 1971. As for "Pavlov," he is the star of the best-selling book *Pavlov's Pad* and appears in other forms from greeting cards to stuffed animals.

Meanwhile, Martin collects Marcel Marceau records (silent, of course) and is married to a woman he modestly claims is the world's most beautiful.

Virgil Partch—On August 12, 1984, the *New York Times* reported a double tragedy: cartoonist Virgil Partch and his wife had died in an automobile accident in California. The creator of "Big George"—who, in the cartoons, seemed to escape unharmed from such incidents as being flattened by an ironing board, blown away by a leaf blower, having a coffee pot parked on his head, and walking down the street while watching TV—had passed away in an all-too-real disaster on the highway.

Virgil Partch was born to a Navy family in Alaska, and he studied at the University of Arizona and the Chouinard Art Institute in Los

Angeles. He sold his first cartoon to *Collier's* magazine in 1942, and after that saw his work published in *The New Yorker, The Saturday Evening Post, Look, True,* and *This Week*. "Big George" was syndicated to newspapers throughout the United States.

Before achieving fame as a cartoonist, Partch worked as an animator at the Disney studios, but a strike put an end to that career. He served in the army in World War II, and some of his humor was drawn from his experiences as a soldier.

His cartoons were collected in a number of books, including *VIP's Quips, New Faces on the Barroom Floor, Bottle Fatigue,* and *Water on the Brain*. A reviewer quoted the publisher's description of Virgil Partch as "America's greatest creator of inspired lunacy."

He will be missed.

Leigh Rubin—Before developing the "Rubes" panel cartoon series, which is currently syndicated and published in a number of major newspapers, including the *Toronto Sun*, the *Detroit Free Press*, the *Denver Post*, the *New York Post*, and the *Sacramento Union*, Leigh Rubin already had a string of successes to his name.

After majoring in advertising art at Pierce College in Woodland Hills, California, he established a publishing company and marketed his own greeting cards. He also published three books between 1981 and 1985: *Notable Quotes, Encore,* and *Amusing Arrangements*, which sold over 70,000 copies and also were the subjects for coffee mugs, greeting cards, and notepads featuring the "Notable" characters.

His fame increased with the publication of *Sharks! . . . Are People Too* and the development of the "Rubes" cartoons, in which characters wrestle with off-the-wall moral and philosophical dilemmas, as well as the challenges of everyday living. *People Magazine* has called the cartoons "sneakily funny" and they have helped earn him the reputation as the "Jay Leno of cartoonists."

All of these things he accomplished by the age of 32!

Harley L. Schwadron—As a graduate of Bowdoin College in Brunswick, Maine, and with a Master of Journalism degree from the University of California in Berkeley, Harley Schwadron was well prepared for his career as newspaper reporter, editor, and public relations staffer. His first newspaper job was as a reporter for the *Hartford Times* in Connecticut. He later became news bureau and alumni magazine editor with the University of Michigan Information Service in Ann Arbor, where he now lives.

But cartooning was always his interest. Even as a Peace Corps volunteer in Thailand, he regularly did cartoons for the *Bangkok World*, and during his 20 years in journalism, he drew his cartoons in the evening hours. Six years ago he became a full-time cartoonist.

His cartoons have appeared in the *Wall Street Journal*, *Playboy*, *Penthouse*, *Omni*, *Good Housekeeping*, and many other publications, including the British comic magazine *Punch*. He also produces the syndicated "Big Biz" cartoon panel that appears in many newspapers and does editorial illustrations for such newspapers as the *Hartford Courant*, *Dayton Daily News*, *Washington Post*, *Washington Times*, and the *St. Paul Pioneer Press*.

He likes to do cartoons that "make a topical statement in a humorous way." Business cartoons have become somewhat of a specialty for him.

Jack Tippit seems to gather honors and awards as fast as just about anybody else in his profession. He received the "Best Magazine Gag Cartoonist of the Year" award from the National Cartoonists Society in 1963 and 1966. The Society also voted his "Amy" cartoon panels "Best Syndicated Cartoon Panel" in 1970. He chaired the Society's Overseas Entertainment Committee from 1966 to 1973, touring hospitals and installations in Vietnam and the Far East with the participation of more than 50 professional cartoonists. He served on the Board of Governors of the National Cartoonists Society from 1967 to 1973, and he is a past director of the Museum of Cartoon Art.

Born in Texas, Tippit received his bachelor of fine arts degree from Syracuse University. After serving 33 years in the U.S. Air Force Reserve, he retired as a full colonel. He saw active Air Force duty in World War II, the Korean War, and Vietnam.

He has created cartoons for leading magazines in the United States and other countries for more than 40 years. His work has appeared in *The New Yorker*, *The Saturday Evening Post*, *Good Housekeeping*, *McCall's*, *Parade*, *Rotarian*, *Ladies' Home Journal*, *Changing Times*, *Family Weekly*, and many other publications.

"Amy" is syndicated by King Features to newspapers throughout the United States, Canada, Iceland, several European countries, and Japan.

A. J. Toos is actually the pen name for a cartooning team. Andrew Grossman thinks up the cartoons in Washington and Jim Toomey, now in San Francisco, does the artwork. Then Grossman markets the results.

Andrew Grossman had ambitions as a writer and a poet. But he also found that he had a sharp sense of humor. So, in 1983, he quit his communications job at a law firm and want into cartooning full time. There was only one problem: he couldn't draw!

The problem was solved by placing an ad. Jim Toomey—almost fresh out of college, and at that time working for the Corcoran Gallery of Art—was lured into becoming the artistic collaborator. Together Grossman and Toomey have produced thousands of cartoons, which Grossman, using the name "A. J. Toos," has sold to the *Washington Post*, the *Boston Globe*, *Reader's Digest*, *The New Yorker*, *The Saturday Evening Post*, *TV Guide*, and other leading publications.

Grossman says the aspiring cartoonist should know his market—what subjects appeal to which publications, and when they want them. A cartoon of a disappointed child at Christmas telling his mother that he wanted a TOY truck (she had gotten him a full-sized one) was sold to the *National Enquirer* in time for their Christmas issue (meaning four months in advance).

"Humor," says Grossman, "is based on two things: ordinary people doing extraordinary things, and extraordinary people doing ordinary things."

There's the secret: now just think up the ideas, draw the cartoons, find out who wants to publish them, and you can also be on the road to success!

If **Jim Unger's** family had been well-to-do, he might today be a professor at Oxford or Cambridge, instead of one of the world's most popular and most successful cartoonists.

If the regular political cartoonist at the *Mississauga Times* had been available, Jim Unger might today still be a competent but ordinary art director at a small-town newspaper.

If somebody had not persuaded Jim Unger to send samples of his cartoons to a newspaper syndicate, he might today be one of the many political cartoonists in Canada.

But instead, Jim Unger's family in London could not afford to send him to college, so he took a series of ordinary jobs. And, growing dissatisfied with his life, Unger migrated to Canada, where he found an art director's job in the advertising department of a small-town newspaper.

And, called upon to fill in when the political cartoonist was sick, Unger's cartoon won an award from the regional newspaper association.

When his sample cartoons arrived at Universal Press Syndicate, they mailed back a ten-year contract. Today "Herman"—the cartoon character named by Universal—appears in 350 newspapers in 24 countries, and over a million copies of "Herman" cartoon collections have been sold. "Herman" was the first comic feature to cross the border to East Germany.

Jim Unger still loves Canada, but his home is in the Bahamas, away from Canadian taxes and cold weather. And, as he says, he gets checks—and plenty of them—"big enough to buy a house with."

Around Home: Losing Your Head Over Television
RUBES® by Leigh Rubin

Quite suddenly and without warning, Herb fell victim to the old adage, "If you don't use it, you lose it."

Key Words

quite	very
without	with no
warning	notice (before something happens)
fell victim to	became a victim of
adage	saying

An Extra Smile

Was Herb beheaded by the boob tube?

1

Around Home: The House Is a Mess
A. J. Toos

"Let's eat out tonight."

Key Words

mess	untidy or cluttered condition
let's	let us; why don't we
eat out	go to a restaurant to eat

An Extra Smile

Of course, if they prefer to dine outdoors, they can just stay where they are!

Around Home: Blowing in the Wind
BIG GEORGE! by Virgil Partch

"I *warned* him about that leaf blower, but you know old George."

Key Words

leaf	growth on a tree
blower	device with a motor that blows air
warned	told in advance

An Extra Smile

George grabbed the leaf blower, and flew off in a rage!

3

Around Home: A Major Breakthrough
A. J. Toos

"I think we've gained a little weight."

Key Words

major	important
breakthrough	act of penetrating a barrier; an advancement
gained	added on
little	not much, a bit
weight	amount in pounds a person weighs

There are millions of overweight Americans—of course these are r-o-u-n-d figures!

At the Office: "All Present Signify by Raising Hands"

Aaron Bacall

"Our first order of business is the problem of absenteeism."

Key Words

all present	everyone here
signify	show, indicate
order of business	item or matter to be discussed
absenteeism	the rate of not going to work regularly

An Extra Smile

Somebody once said that a meeting is where people take minutes and waste hours!

At the Office: Smoker's Last Stand
Harley L. Schwadron

"Relax, Ms. Wayne, I'm not going to jump. I came out here to smoke."

Key Words

smoker	person who smokes cigarettes
last stand	final resort
relax	calm yourself
Ms.	form of address for women (without reference to marital status)
came out	left the building

An Extra Smile

People used to ask smokers to put out their cigarettes—now they just put out the smokers!

At the Office: Advice from Behind Bars
BRIEFCASE by John Louthan

© 1990 Universal Press Syndicate   7-24   LOUTHAN

"You bet you can write off your Hawaiian vacation."

Key Words

behind bars	in jail
you bet	certainly, sure
write off	subtract from one's taxes

An Extra Smile

That accountant is on vacation now—in jail!

At the Office: Testing the Product
Harley L. Schwadron

"They're in conference at the moment."

Key Words

testing	trying out
grandma	informal for "grandmother"
Co.	abbreviation of "Company"
in conference	in a business meeting
at the moment	now, this minute

An Extra Smile

Pie is not fattening the way they serve it in restaurants—the pieces are too small!

At the Office: Just Give Me the Facts (Fax), Ma'am
PAVLOV® by Ted Martin

Key Words

just	only
"gimme"	conversational for "give me"
Ma'am	short for "Madam," a form of polite address
fax	facsimile machine
unplug	pull out the electric plug or cord

An Extra Smile

Max, the tax on the fax is hard on our "bax"!

At the Office: Knowing His Place
Harley L. Schwadron

"Goodwin, will you get down from there?"

Key Words

corporate	of a company or corporation
headquarters	main office
get down	come down

An Extra Smile

The map says "You are here," and Goodwin REALLY is there!

At the Office: Steps to Success
Harley L. Schwadron

"As you all know, I've stepped on a lot of people on my way to the top."

Key Words

step	stride; stage in a process
stepped on	took advantage of; abused the goodwill of

An Extra Smile

Instead of standing on his record, he's standing on his assistant!

At the Office: Phone in the Field
Henry Martin

"The portable phone has made it possible for me to set up business just about anywhere."

Key Words

portable	able to be carried
phone	short for "telephone"
to set up	to conduct, carry on
just about	almost

An Extra Smile

You can tell a person anything, but you can't tell-a-phone!

At the Office: File and Forget
Harley L. Schwadron

"Why, Mr. Overmayer! What in heaven's name are you doing in the 'M' file?"

Key Words

file and forget	do nothing about something
Mr.	abbreviation for "Mister"
in heaven's name	exclamation of surprise

An Extra Smile

It's bad enough to be found in the filing cabinet, but unforgivable to be found under the wrong letter!

At the Office: Getting a Lift from the Boss
Harley L. Schwadron

"I promised you a raise, Jones—but I never promised it would be in the form of money."

Key Words

getting a lift from	feeling happy about
raise	an increase in salary

An Extra Smile

The boss has jacked up everything except Mr. Jones' spirits!

At the Office: Bright Ideas
Henry Martin

"Luckily, we have a tremendous flow of ideas going through here."

Key Words

bright	smart, useful
tremendous	large in amount or number
flow	stream, outpouring

An Extra Smile

Just be careful not to break any of those light bulbs!

At the Office: Pajama Party
Harley L. Schwadron

"Congratulations, Harwell! You finally made it to work on time."

Key Words

pajamas	clothing to wear while sleeping
made it to	arrived at; came to
on time	at the correct hour

An Extra Smile

Now that he's made it to the office, he's ready for a good nap!

At the Office: Pull Yourself Together
Henry Martin

A TYPICAL BUSINESS SITUATION

3-15

"Ed's grounded in Newark. His audio-visuals are in Chicago. His meeting in Atlanta starts in 15 minutes. Now, here's my plan . . ."

Key Words

grounded	forced to stay on the ground when traveling by airplane
audio-visuals	recordings, charts, etc.

An Extra Smile

A young man once complained that his girlfriend broke his heart in three places—Kansas City, Chicago, and New York!

At the Office: Hammock Deluxe
Harley L. Schwadron

"No one has seen Mr. Wilfogle all morning."

Key Words

deluxe

all morning

luxurious

during the entire morning

An Extra Smile

Let's just hope he doesn't start snoring!

18

Baby: Spin the Baby
A. J. Toos

"Honey, you're not playing rough with the baby, are you?"

Key Words

honey	affectionate form of address
playing rough	playing in a very physical or dangerous way

An Extra Smile

Babies make the world go 'round—or is it the OTHER way around?

Birds: This Is for the Birds
A. J. Toos

"You just had to have a birdfeeder!"

Key Words

had to have — insisted on owning

birdfeeder — a device that one fills with seeds for birds to eat

An Extra Smile

A bird in the bush is worth 100 birds hanging around the house!

Birds: Can You Spare a Dime?
BIG GEORGE! by Virgil Partch

"Forget the popcorn. This one only accepts hard cash."

Key Words

spare   give easily

dime   ten-cent coin

forget   don't bother with

accepts   takes

hard cash   coins, paper currency, or money

An Extra Smile

He probably won't take a credit card either!

Birds: Crying Fowl
BIG GEORGE! by Virgil Partch

"I don't know when I've heard a sadder rendition of 'Happy Days Are Here Again.' "

Key Words

fowl	bird
rendition	performance; way of playing (on an instrument)

An Extra Smile

That's no rendition! The bird is **rending** the tune—note by note.

Books: A "How-to" Book
THE BETTER HALF® by Jay Harris

HARRIS 11-24

© 1990 by Cowles Syndicate, Inc.

"You don't read this book—you stand on it."

Key Words

"how-to" book

a book with instructions on how to do something

An Extra Smile

Does he really want to be taller, or did somebody put him up to it?

Books: The Late Guest Speaker
HERMAN® by Jim Unger

© 1991 Jim Unger/Distributed by Universal Press Syndicate

"He's probably held up in traffic."

Key Words

late	tardy; dead
the mob	a gang of criminals
held up	delayed; accosted and robbed
traffic	cars, trucks, etc., on a road

An Extra Smile

Or was he held up by another member of the mob?

Courtship: She's His Means of Support
A. J. Toos

"You bring out the little boy in me!"

Key Words

means of support	source of money
means	method, way
support	to hold up, carry
bring out	make me feel like; encourage

An Extra Smile

Maybe he wants to pursue her until she catches him!

Courtship: Being Handsome Saves Money
HERMAN® by Jim Unger

4/25

©1989 Universal Press Syndicate

"Money or good looks attract me. I'd say you'd need about $15 million."

money	wealth; fortune
attract me	make me interested
I'd say	I would estimate or guess

But isn't true love priceless?

Dentists: At the Dentist
BIG GEORGE! by Virgil Partch

"Well, George, what seems to be your problem?"

Key Words

seems	appears
problem	difficulty

An Extra Smile

The dentist is carrying enough electric tools to build a bookcase!

Dentists: Sweet Dreams!
TRUDY by Jerry Marcus

"Remember, you've got a dental appointment first thing in the morning."

Key Words

sweet	pleasant, enjoyable
remember	recall, do not forget
got	have
dental appointment	visit to the dentist's office
first thing	at the earliest time

An Extra Smile

Relax—you've only your teeth to lose!

Driving: The Movable Clothesline
HERMAN® by Jim Unger

© 1989 Universal Press Syndicate

5/19

"What is it this time?"

Key Words

movable — able to be moved

clothesline — cord on which clothes are hung to dry

An Extra Smile

Do you think the driver's been in trouble with this police officer before?

Driving: How to Save Money with a Trojan Horse
WARP FACTOR by Karlos Barney

"Are you *sure* there's only two of you in there?"

Key Words

drive-in   place to watch movies from inside your car

sure   certain, positive

An Extra Smile

What would they do if a wooden horse wasn't allowed in?

Driving: Flat Tire
TRUDY by Jerry Marcus

"The 'bumper jack'? Is that the metal thing I use as a doorstop in my laundry room?"

Key Words

flat tire	tire with no air in it
bumper jack	device for lifting up a car
doorstop	heavy object used to hold open a door
laundry	clothing and other things to be washed

An Extra Smile

But what would Trudy do to hold the laundry room door open if Dad had taken the bumper jack?

Driving: Warning to Drunk Drivers
WARP FACTOR by Karlos Barney

© 1990 Creators Syndicate, Inc. 12-1

"Sarge, isn't your new sobriety test a bit harsh?"

Key Words

sarge	informal, short form of "sergeant"
sobriety	state of being sober (not having drunk alcoholic beverages)
harsh	cruel, hard

An Extra Smile

You wouldn't want to have to "string along" with Sarge!

Driving: No Standing
BIG GEORGE! by Virgil Partch

"It looks as if you've picked up another parking ticket."

Key Words

looks	seems, appears
picked up	received
ticket	fine issued by police for breaking a law or rule

An Extra Smile

When the meter maid wrote the parking ticket, she had to find SOMEPLACE to leave it!

Driving: Making a Clean Job of It
BRIEFCASE by John Luthan

©1990 Universal Press Syndicate

REPAIR

LOUTHAN 3·31

"I'll be in the shower with your carburetor."

Key Words

make a clean job of it	to do something well
shower	stall with spraying water for bathing
carburetor	device that mixes fuel and air and supplies the mixture to the engine

An Extra Smile

After an expensive carburetor repair the driver's wallet will be cleaned out, too!

Driving: Special Delivery
HERMAN® by Jim Unger

1/14 © 1991 Jim Unger/Distributed by Universal Press Syndicate

"Just imagine I'm a pizza and deliver me to my sister's."

Key Words

special	not ordinary
imagine	pretend, form a mental image
deliver	take
sister's	sister's house

An Extra Smile

A pizza has been described as "a flying saucer with cheese"!

Driving: Intensive Care
PAVLOV® by Ted Martin

© 1989 Universal Press Syndicate   3-22

"How . . . how serious is it?"

Key Words

intensive   extremely dedicated

serious   grave, critical

An Extra Smile

The driver should jack up the license plate and put a new car under it!

Driving: Getaway Car
Harley L. Schwadron

"I wish to report a runaway car."

Key Words

getaway	escape
wish	want
to report	to announce, to inform someone of something
runaway	fugitive, escaped

An Extra Smile

She should be happy her car still runs!

Driving: Cliffhanger
PAVLOV® by Ted Martin

Sign: "Last Gas for 5,000 ft."

Key Words

cliffhanger	suspenseful or tense situation
gas	gasoline
ft.	abbreviation for "feet"

An Extra Smile

Maybe there's a gas station at the bottom of the cliff with a sign that says: "Drop In Any Time"!

Guests: No Bowling Tonight
TRUDY by Jerry Marcus

10-13

Jerry Marcus

"It wasn't easy to persuade Ed to come . . . it's his bowling night."

Key Words

to persuade   to convince, to talk into doing

An Extra Smile

Is Ed carrying his bowling ball as a protest—or are his fingers caught in it?

Guests: Smile and the World Smiles with You
A. J. Toos

"Frank never smiles when he's really having fun."

Key Words

world	all the people
really	truly, in fact
having fun	enjoying himself

An Extra Smile

Remember: happiness is no laughing matter!

Guests: Forgotten Invitation
TRUDY by Jerry Marcus

"Did you invite the Pratts over for dinner tonight?"

Key Words

forgotten   not remembered

invite over   ask to come to one's house

An Extra Smile

Maybe they can say that the dog ate their appointment calendar

Guests: Unexpected Guests
TRUDY by Jerry Marcus

jerrymarcus

"Remember? The Bradleys' party? You guys said, 'If you're ever in the neighborhood, just drop by!' "

Key Words

unexpected	not planned; not anticipated
guys	informal, slang for "people"
ever	at any time
neighborhood	area where one lives
drop by	visit (without calling in advance)

An Extra Smile

Maybe they can pretend that everyone else from the Bradley's party is ALREADY staying at their house!

Husbands and Wives: Answering the Call
BIG GEORGE! by Virgil Partch

"I wonder who could be calling at this hour?"

Key Words

answering the call	picking up the telephone when it rings; responding to a summons
wonder	ask oneself
calling	telephoning, making a telephone call
hour	time of day or night

An Extra Smile

If that coffeepot is really hot, George is going to get a new hairdo!

Husbands and Wives: He's Flat Out for Exercise
Aaron Bacall

"He spent two thousand dollars on gym equipment and all he ever exercises is caution."

Key Words

flat out	going full speed
spent on	paid (money) for
gym	short for "gymnasium"
equipment	machines, set of apparatus
all	the only thing
exercises	puts into action
caution	care, precaution

An Extra Smile

This cartoon really shows the difference between "flat out" enthusiasm and "out flat" relaxation!

Husbands and Wives: Straight Tie
BIG GEORGE! by Virgil Partch

"It's a nice job, but I think there's a bit too much starch in it for my taste."

Key Words

nice	good, well done
job	piece of work
starch	substance used to stiffen material
taste	preference

An Extra Smile

Maybe George can use the tie as a propeller . . .

Husbands and Wives: Happy Opinion
HERMAN® by Jim Unger

"He said I don't need glasses!"

Key Words

glasses	eyeglasses, usually prescribed by an optometrist or eye doctor
optimist	person who considers only the good or positive

An Extra Smile

An optometrist is someone who prescribes rose-colored glasses for an optimist.

Husbands and Wives: TV En Route
BIG GEORGE! by Virgil Partch

"Careful now, there's a curb here. How's the game coming?"

Key Words

en route	on the way
careful	be cautious
curb	raised side of the street
coming	progressing

An Extra Smile

Everything will probably be fine until George tries to applaud a touchdown.

Husbands and Wives: Hard on the Teeth
WARP FACTOR by Karlos Barney

"Gee, look what I found while I was looking for the cordless screwdriver."

Key Words

hard	bad, destructive
gee	exclamation, similar to "oh!"
found	located
while	during the time
looking for	trying to find
cordless	without a cord; operated on batteries

An Extra Smile

And I wonder what he's using for toothpaste!

Husbands and Wives: Jogging the Memory
A. J. Toos

"That reminds me. Happy Anniversary."

Key Words

jogging the memory	reminding someone
reminds	helps to remember
anniversary	yearly celebration of a wedding

An Extra Smile

Is it true that the greatest surprise a husband can give his wife on their anniversary is remembering it?

Husbands and Wives: Unhappy Wife
THE BETTER HALF® by Jay Harris

"Harriet is a little moody today."

Key Words

unhappy	not pleased
moody	not happy, temperamental

An Extra Smile

It's really a happy marriage—she loves him, and he loves him!

Husbands and Wives: Bored with Ironing
BIG GEORGE! by Virgil Partch

"Well, you DID want me to iron a shirt for you, didn't you?"

Key Words

bored	not interested
to iron	to remove wrinkles with an iron; to press

An Extra Smile

George should try ironing his own shirts!

Husbands and Wives: Postal Poverty
HERMAN® by Jim Unger

10/1

© 1990 Universal Press Syndicate

"I wrote you love letters before we were married because I could afford stamps."

Key Words

postal	of the mail
poverty	state of being poor
because	for the reason that
afford	have enough money for
stamps	postage for sending mail

An Extra Smile

He has very creative excuses!

Husbands and Wives: Getting His Attention
BIG GEORGE! by Virgil Partch

"All right, all right! Now that you have my attention, what's on your mind?"

Key Words

all right	OK
attention	full awareness
on your mind	thinking about

An Extra Smile

When her foot is on his chest, he's anxious to know what's on her mind!

Husbands and Wives: Eating in Bed
TRUDY by Jerry Marcus

"How about half of this onion-garlic sandwich?"

Key Words

how about	would you like
half	one of two equal parts

An Extra Smile

Even if he doesn't take half of the sandwich, the fragrance is going to keep him awake!

Husbands and Wives: Interrupting a Phone Call
BIG GEORGE! by Virgil Partch

"Oh, you've got a cordless phone? I tried to talk George into getting one, but you know George."

Key Words

got	have
cordless phone	telephone with a receiver not connected by a cord
to talk into	to convince, persuade
getting	buying; acquiring

An Extra Smile

In a moment George is going to see why he should have bought a cordless phone.

In the Courtroom: Putting the Jury to the Test
BRIEFCASE by John Louthan

"It's unanimous, Your Honor: They think I look more believable in my gray pinstripe."

Key Words

putting to the test	trying out
unanimous	agreed, all having the same opinion
Your Honor	form of addressing a judge
believable	dependable, credible
pinstripe	suit of material with evenly spaced narrow stripes

An Extra Smile

This lawyer pays for his suits by winning suits in court!

In the Courtroom: Case Dismissed
HERMAN® by Jim Unger

10/2

© 1990 Universal Press Syndicate

"I've decided to give you another chance. Next time case the joint first."

Key Words

decided	concluded, reached a decision
chance	opportunity
case the joint	slang: examine the place carefully

An Extra Smile

Do you think the judge wants a share of the loot?

Kids: Billy Got Carried Away
WARP FACTOR by Karlos Barney

"Now where's that little Billy? He was just here a minute ago blowing bubbles."

Key Words

carried away	taken away
get carried away	to become overly excited
just here	in this spot
a minute ago	a short time in the past
blowing bubbles	making bubbles by blowing on soapy liquid

An Extra Smile

Billy loved blowing bubbles so much he really got carried away!

Kids: Don't Look Now
A. J. Toos

"And what have you two been doing all day?"

Key Words

you two	both of you
all day	during the entire day

An Extra Smile

"Hey, Mom, whatever we've been doing, it's no big thing!"

Kids: Young Surgeon
AMY® by Jack Tippit

"I brought along a surgery specialist . . . jus' in case we have to cut anything out."

Key Words

surgeon	doctor who performs operations
brought along	took with
specialist	expert on a specific subject
jus'	just
have to	must
cut out	remove with a knife

An Extra Smile

When Dad says "Cut it out!" we hope the kids don't misunderstand . . .

Kids: Sharing the Dirt
AMY® by Jack Tippit

© 1990 by Cowles Syndicate, Inc.

8-29

"Thanks, anyway, Denny . . . but I *wouldn't* care for a li'l bite of your cookie."

Key Words

sharing	giving a part of one's possession
sharing the dirt	gossiping
Thanks, anyway	Thank you, but no
care for	like
li'l	little

An Extra Smile

Denny sure likes to "dish out the dirt."

Kids: Girl Plumber
AMY® by Jack Tippit

© 1990 by Cowles Syndicate, Inc.

9-7

"I'm thinkin' 'bout bein' a plumber, Mr. Mandy. Where do I start?"

Key Words

plumber	person who works with or repairs water pipes
thinkin'	thinking; considering
'bout	about
bein'	being
start	begin

An Extra Smile

The answer is obvious—under the sink!

Kids: Smart Scale
AMY® by Jack Tippit

"You are kind, generous, and honest . . . and you're late for your piano lesson."

Key Words

scale	device for measuring weight
kind	gentle, loving
generous	of a giving nature
honest	truthful
fortune	fate, what will happen in the future

An Extra Smile

Instead of the piano lesson, the **scale** is teaching Amy a lesson!

Kids: Burnt Offering
AMY® by Jack Tippit

"Is lemon meringue pie s'posed to be black on top?"

Key Words

burnt	having been burned
meringue	topping made of whipped egg whites
s'posed	"supposed"; ought

An Extra Smile

It's the thought that counts!

Kids: Call-Waiting
TRUDY by Jerry Marcus

"I got *four* at this end! How many do you have?"

Key Words

at this end   here

An Extra Smile

This is NOT what the telephone company means when it offers call-waiting service!

Kids: Outsmarting the Parents
TRUDY by Jerry Marcus

"I say let's stay one step ahead of 'em!"

Key Words

psychology	study of individual behavior
outsmarting	winning by being more clever
let's	let us
ahead	in front
'em	them

An Extra Smile

The kids will learn to behave "by the book"!

Kids: It's a Zoo in There!
AMY® by Jack Tippit

"DON'T OPEN THAT DOOR, MOM!"

Key Words

zoo	park where animals are displayed; messy; disorganized place
mom	mother

An Extra Smile

But the door can't stay closed forever . . .

Mealtime: Instant Thanksgiving
Aaron Bacall

"For the turkey-helper, the one-minute rice, the instant mashed potato mix, the heat and serve cranberry pudding, and the quick fix instant stuffing, this working mother is truly thankful."

Key Words

turkey-helper	mixture for preparing turkey more quickly
mix	package of ingredients
quick fix	prepare fast
stuffing	mixture that is cooked inside the turkey
truly	really, truthfully
thankful	grateful

An Extra Smile

The problem with some of these instant foods is instant indigestion!

Mealtime: Home-Brewed Coffee
WARP FACTOR by Karlos Barney

Pouring the coffee through grandpa's beard removed the caffeine alright, but it kept the old man up for days at a time.

Key Words

home-brewed	made at home
grandpa	informal for "grandfather"
removed	took out
caffeine	substance used as a stimulant to make people alert
alright	all right, definitely
kept up	did not allow to sleep
at a time	in one period

An Extra Smile

You'd have trouble sleeping, too, if you went to bed every night with a wet beard.

Kids: Pounding the Table
A. J. Toos

"This isn't about eating my peas, this is about the struggle of men everywhere to throw off the yoke of tyranny."

Key Words

pounding	hitting
isn't about	does not deal with
struggle	fight, difficult effort
to throw off	to remove by force
yoke	device used to restrain or keep in place
tyranny	rule by a tyrant or dictator

An Extra Smile

Bet George Washington's army ate their peas!

Mealtime: When Smoke Gets in Your Eyes
THE BETTER HALF® by Jay Harris

"Here's a little cooking hint for you. The smoke alarm should *not* be used as a timer."

Key Words

hint	suggestion
alarm	device for warning
as	in the place of
timer	device for measuring length of time

An Extra Smile

Where there's smoke, the cook should get fired!

Mealtime: In a Pickle
THE BETTER HALF® by Jay Harris

"I couldn't find a banana for your cereal, so I used a cucumber."

Key Words

pickle	vegetable, usually a cucumber, processed in vinegar
in a pickle	in trouble
cereal	breakfast food made of grains such as rice, wheat, corn, etc.
so	thus, therefore

An Extra Smile

Don't accept an invitation to breakfast at THEIR house.

Mealtime: Coffee . . . with a Punch
THE BETTER HALF® by Jay Harris

"It's a new kind of coffee cup—it wakes up decaf drinkers."

Key Words

punch	a blow with a fist
with a punch	with added zest
kind	type
wakes up	rouses from sleep
decaf	short for "decaffeinated"
drinkers	people who drink

An Extra Smile

But it might take more than a punch to wake HIM up!

Mealtime: At the Breakfast Table
THE BETTER HALF® by Jay Harris

"Even though I ignore you every morning, you still sit here with me. You're a wonderful wife, Harriet."

Key Words

even though	in spite of the fact that; although
ignore	do not pay attention to
still	always, yet
wonderful	very good, magnificent

An Extra Smile

I hope "Harriet" doesn't pop!

Mealtime: Breaking the Diet
THE BETTER HALF® by Jay Harris

© 1990 by Cowles Syndicate, Inc.

HARRIS 10-19

"The Two-Week Diet turned out to be a *too weak* diet."

Key Words

diet	plan for losing weight
turned out	resulted in
too	very
weak	not strong; feeble

An Extra Smile

He's "fed up" with his diet!

Mealtime: Restaurant Filling Station
PAVLOV® by Ted Martin

Key Words

filling station   gas or service station

An Extra Smile

It looks as though they sell coffee by the gallon!

On the Job: It's a Dog-Eat-Dog World!
BIG GEORGE! by Virgil Partch

"The competition will stop at nothing."

Key Words

dog-eat-dog	competitive
competition	opponent (in business or sports)
stop at nothing	do anything necessary to achieve a goal

An Extra Smile

Sorry George, you'll have to wait. He's all tied up!

On the Job: Formula for a Sure Thing
Aaron Bacall

"Assuming, of course, that they don't change jockeys before the race."

Key Words

formula	equation for solving a problem
sure thing	something that cannot fail or lose
assuming	guessing, supposing
of course	naturally, surely
jockeys	riders (on race horses)

An Extra Smile

Horses are too smart to bet on people, but the opposite is not true!

On the Job: Stone Age Office Supplies
RUBES® by Leigh Rubin

It was highly doubtful that Gorg would ever attain commercial success in his lifetime.

Key Words

Stone Age	prehistoric time
office supplies	items needed in an office
highly	very, extremely
doubtful	uncertain, unlikely
attain	reach, gain
commercial	relating to business
lifetime	length of a person's life

An Extra Smile

This reminds us of the doctor who told the cave man to take two "tablets" and call him in the morning.

On the Job: I Don't Know Much About Art, but . . .
WARP FACTOR by Karlos Barney

© 1991 Creators Syndicate, Inc.

Karlos Barney
1-8

"My secret? I just chip away everything that doesn't look like a marble countertop."

Key Words

chip	knock off little pieces
look like	appear to be
marble	hard, smooth stone
countertop	covering of a cabinet or counter

An Extra Smile

Michelangelo's "David" lives—as a kitchen sink!

On the Job: The See-Through Soldier
WARP FACTOR by Karlos Barney

"Fortunately, just as I was choking on a piece of jerky, a stray cannonball cleared my airway."

Key Words

see-through	transparent; with a hole for looking through
jerky	dried beef
stray	off course
cannonball	round, solid ball shot from a cannon
airway	tube from the nose and mouth to the lungs

An Extra Smile

Wouldn't a slap on the back have been more comfortable?

On the Job: Along Came a Spider
WARP FACTOR by Karlos Barney

1991 Creators Syndicate. Inc.

"If *I* didn't install a new safety net, and *you* didn't . . . then who did?"

Key Words

install   set up, put in place

safety   for protection against injury

An Extra Smile

What does the spider have in mind if one of them falls into the net?

On the Job: Hold the Line
Harley L. Schwadron

"Arlene, how many times have I told you not to call me at work?"

Key Words

hold the line	wait
to call	to telephone

An Extra Smile

How did Arlene know where to phone him?

On the Job: Funny Money
Henry Martin

©1991 Tribune Media Services, Inc.
All Rights Reserved

"I want to turn in a $16 bill that I suspect is counterfeit."

Key Words

funny	strange, unusual
funny money	counterfeit bills
to turn in	to give to the authorities
suspect	think something is wrong
counterfeit	false

An Extra Smile

By the way, it's the Secret Service not the FBI that goes after counterfeiters.

Pets: In the Doghouse
A. J. Toos

"Come to bed, Arthur. You're forgiven, and besides, Bowzer is shivering."

Key Words

in the doghouse	figurative for "in trouble"
forgiven	pardoned, excused
besides	also, in addition
shivering	shaking from the cold

An Extra Smile

Has she really forgiven Arthur, or did Bowzer talk her into it to get his doghouse back?

Pets: When the Cat's Away
A. J. Toos

"And then one day I just lost my taste for mice."

Key Words

lost	could not find
taste	liking, enjoyment
mice	plural of mouse

An Extra Smile

Maybe she should try the broom on those lazy cats!

Pets: Starting from Scratch
A. J. Toos

"This itch behind my ear is driving me crazy. Could you give me a hand?"

Key Words

start from scratch	to begin a task
scratch	to scrape with the fingernails
	to relieve an itch
itch	irritation
driving	making
crazy	mentally unbalanced
give a hand	help

An Extra Smile

You scratch his back, he'll scratch yours!

Pets: Read the Label First
A. J. Toos

"Let's see here. It says 'These biscuits will help your puppy grow into a strong, healthy, ten-foot high dog'."

Key Words

label	sign on a package
biscuits	hard crackers
puppy	young dog
grow into	become

An Extra Smile

Talk about creating a monster!

Pets: Leaving Home
A. J. Toos

"Why didn't you tell me you're just going on a vacation! I thought you were trying to move without me!"

Key Words

vacation	trip
to move	to change homes

An Extra Smile

They just wanted a "doggone" vacation!

Pets: Cat Food
TRUDY by Jerry Marcus

FATKAT

8-22

Jerry Marcus

"Eat that or I'll give it to Daddy!"

Key Words

daddy   affectionate term for "father"

An Extra Smile

Who's treated better in this house?

Pets: Dog-Tired
AMY® by Jack Tippit

"Rosemary, I think we're outta gas."

Key Words

dog-tired	very tired
outta	"out of"; have no more of
gas	fuel

An Extra Smile

Talk about laying down on the job!

Pets: The Dog's Chair
TRUDY by Jerry Marcus

"When I say *'sit'*, I don't mean in my chair!"

Key Words

mean   intend to say

An Extra Smile

The command to "sit" is just one of those things dogs won't stand for.

Pets: House-broken Mouse
BIG GEORGE! by Virgil Partch

"Relax! It's only a toy!"

Key Words

only
toy

nothing but
something to play with

An Extra Smile

But toys are supposed to be fun!

Shipwreck: Noah's Miscalculation
WARP FACTOR by Karlos Barney

11-21   © 1990 Creators Syndicate, Inc.

"Are you sure 'two of everything' included termites?"

Key Words

miscalculation	error
included	meant to have as part of something
termites	members of the ant family that feed on wood

An Extra Smile

A new version of the Biblical story—Noah took two termites on the ark and they ate it!

Shipwreck: A Swimming Vacation
HERMAN® by Jim Unger

"My doctor told me to take a cruise and relax."

Key Words

to take	to go on
a cruise	a trip on a large ship
relax	rest

An Extra Smile

Folks on that ship must have had a sinking feeling!

Shipwreck: King of the Sand Castle
RUBES® by Leigh Rubin

Although he was officially referred to as "exalted lord and master of all he surveyed," it was largely a ceremonial position.

Key Words

officially	according to authorities
referred to	called
exalted	admired, worshipped
surveyed	saw, inspected
largely	mostly
ceremonial	for celebrations
position	job

An Extra Smile

Notice the ceremonial position—leaning against the tree!

Shipwreck: Now for a Shopping List
WARP FACTOR by Karlos Barney

"Because of your excellent credit history, you have been selected to receive a pre-approved credit card . . ."

Key Words

because	as a result of
excellent	very good
credit history	record of how well one has paid bills in the past
selected	chosen
pre-approved	approved in advance

An Extra Smile

He'll have to send the bottle back with a message asking what his credit limit will be.

Sports: Gulliver Tops the Score
RUBES® by Leigh Rubin

Creators Syndicate, Inc
©1990 Leigh Rubin

"It's my pleasure to extend you a warm welcome on behalf of all the fine citizens of Lilliput...especially our basketball team!"

Key Words

pleasure	happy task
to extend	to offer
warm	sincere, friendly
on behalf of	as representative of
especially	above all
basketball	game played on a court with a ball and hoops
team	group of players

An Extra Smile

The team should win every game now—unless Gulliver accidently swallows their basketball.

Travel: In the Baggage Claim
BRIEFCASE by John Louthan

"This is no way to come back from Vegas."

Key Words

baggage	luggage; suitcases
claim	area for receiving (one's luggage)
no way	not a good method
to come back	to return home
Vegas	Las Vegas (Nevada)

An Extra Smile

Las Vegas: also known as "Lost Wages," Nevada.

Weather: A Wet Wetsuit
BIG GEORGE! by Virgil Partch

"It's really coming down out there."

Key Words

wetsuit	outfit worn by scuba divers
coming down	raining hard
out there	outside

An Extra Smile

George doesn't like to use umbrellas!

Weather: Gone with the Snow
Harley L. Schwadron

"Marvin, where's the car?"

Key Words

gone	not in sight
snow	precipitation in winter

An Extra Smile

Maybe Marvin should move to Florida!

Glossary

NOTE: Many words have a number of different meanings. A meaning given here relates only to the meaning of the word or phrase as it is used on the cartoon page. You may find additional meanings and explanations in the section **Points of Interest,** following the glossary. Other words can be found in the beginning sections of this book.

about almost, more or less, 26

absenteeism the rate of not going to work regularly, 5

accepts takes, 21

adage saying, proverb, 1

advice helpful suggestion, 7

afford have enough money for, 52

again once more, 22

ahead in front of, 66

airway tube from the nose and mouth to the lungs, 81

alarm device for warning, 71

all the only thing, 44; everything, 96

all day during the entire day, 59

all morning during the entire morning, 18

all present everyone here, 5

all right OK, 53; definitely, 69

although in spite of the fact, even though, 96

anniversary yearly celebration of a wedding, 49

another one more, 33, 57

answering responding to, 43

anywhere in any place, 12

as in the place of, 71

assuming guessing, supposing, 78

at a time in one period, 69

attain reach, gain, 79

attention full awareness, 53

at this end here, 65

attract me make me interested, 26

audio-visuals recordings, charts, etc., 17

baby infant, very young child, 19

baggage luggage, suitcase, 99

banana long, yellow fruit, 72

bars, behind in jail, 7

basketball game played on a court with a ball and hoops, 98

beard hair grown on the face, 69

because for the reason that, 52; as a result of, 97

before prior to the time, 52, 78

behalf of, on as representative of, 98

believable dependable, credible, 56

besides also, in addition, 85

bet, you certainly, sure, 7

birdfeeder   a device that one fills with seeds for birds to eat, 20

birds   creatures with feathered wings, 20

biscuits   hard crackers, 88

bit, a   just a little, 32, 45

bite   a small taste, 61

blower   device with a motor that blows air, 3

blowing bubbles   making bubbles by blowing on soapy liquid, 58

bored   not interested in, 51

boss   a person's supervisor or employer, 14

bowling   a game played by knocking over pins with a ball, 39

boy   a young male child, 25

breakfast   the morning meal, 72

breaking   stopping, 75

breakthrough   act of penetrating a barrier; an advancement, 4

bright   smart, useful, 15

bring out   make me feel like, encourage, 25

brought along   took with, 60

bumper jack   device for lifting up a car, 31

burnt   having been burned, 64

caffeine   substance used as a stimulant to keep people alert, 69

call   telephone call, 43, 55

call, to   to make a telephone call, 83

calling   telephoning, making a telephone call, 43

came out   left the building, 6

cannonball   round, solid ball shot from a cannon, 81

car   automobile, 37, 101

carburetor   device that mixes fuel and air and supplies it to the engine, 34

care   treatment, 36

care for   like, 61

careful   be cautious, 47

carried away   taken away, 58

case   legal case, 57

case the joint   slang: examine the place carefully, 57

castle, sand   palace made of sand on a beach, 96

caution   care, precaution, 44

cereal   breakfast food made of grains such as rice, wheat, corn, etc., 72

ceremonial   for celebrations, 96

chance   opportunity, 57

change   make a substitution, 78

chip   knock off little pieces, 80

choking   having something stuck in the throat, 81

citizens   residents, 98

claim   area for receiving (one's luggage), 99

cleared   removed the obstacle, 81

cliffhanger suspenseful or tense situation, 38

clothesline cord on which clothes are hung to dry, 29

Co. abbreviation of "Company," 8

coffee drink made of coffee beans, 69, 73

come, to to go along, 39, 85

come back, to to return home, 99

coming progressing, 47

coming down raining hard, 100

commercial relating to business, 79

competition opponent (in business or sports), 77

conference, in in a business meeting, 8

congratulations exclamation of praise, 16

cookie a dessert or sweet snack, 61

cooking preparing food, 71

cordless without a cord; operated on batteries, 48, 55

corporate of a company or corporation, 10

counterfeit false, phony, 84

countertop covering of a cabinet or counter, 80

crazy mentally unbalanced, 87

credit card card with which to buy something now and pay for it later, 97

credit history record of how well one has paid bills in the past, 97

cruise a trip on a large ship, 95

crying crying out; weeping, shedding tears, 22

cucumber crispy, green vegetable, 72

cup mug or container for drinking, 73

curb raised side of the street, 47

cut out remove with a knife, 60

daddy affectionate term for "father," 90

decaf short for "decaffeinated," 73

decided concluded, reached a decision, 57

deliver take, 35

deluxe first-class, elegant, 18

dental appointment visit to the dentist's office, 28

dentist doctor who fixes teeth, 27

diet plan for losing weight, 75

dime ten-cent coin, 21

dinner the evening meal, 41

dirt dust and soil, 61

dismissed released, let go, 57

doctor physician, 95

doorstop heavy object used to hold open a door, 31

dog-eat-dog world ferocious society, 77

doubtful   uncertain, unlikely, 79

drinkers   people who drink, 73

drive-in (movies)   place to watch movies from inside your car, 30

drivers   people who drive cars, 32

driving   making, 87

drop by   visit (without calling in advance), 42

drunk   being impaired by alcohol, 32

easy   simple, 39

eat out   go to a restaurant, 2

en route   on the way, 47

equipment   machines, set of apparatus, 44

especially   above all, 98

even though   in spite of the fact that, although, 74

ever   at any time, 42, 44

every   each, 74

everything   all things, 94

exalted   admired, worshipped, 96

excellent   very good, 97

exercise   physical activity, 44

exercises   puts into action, 44

extend, to   to offer, 98

facts   data, true events, 9

fax   facsimile machine, 9

fell victim to   became a victim of, 1

field, in the   away from the office, 12

file   a file folder or file drawer, 13

file and forget   do nothing about something, 13

filling station   gas or service station, 76

finally   at last, in the end, 16

find   locate, 72

fine   good, 98

first thing   at the earliest time, 28

flat out   going full speed, 44

flat tire   tire with no air in it, 31

flow   stream, outpouring, 15

forget   not remember, 13; don't bother with, 21

forgiven   pardoned, excused, 85

forgotten   not remembered, 41

form   shape, appearance, 14

formula   equation for solving a problem, 78

fortunately   with good luck, 81

fortune   fate, what will happen in the future, 63

found   located, 48

fowl   bird, 22

ft.   abbreviation for "feet," 38

funny   strange, unusual, 84

gained   added on, 4

game   sporting event, 47

gas   gasoline, 38; fuel, 91

gee   exclamation, similar to "oh!", 48

generous   of a giving nature, 63

getaway escape, 37

get down come down, climb down, 10

getting acquiring, 53; buying, 55

getting a lift from feeling happy about, 14

girl a young female child, 62

give tell, 9; offer, 57, 90

give a hand help, 87

glasses eyeglasses, usually prescribed by an optometrist or eye doctor, 46

going leaving, 89

gone not in sight, 101

got have, 28, 55, 65

grandma informal for "grandmother," 8

grandpa informal for "grandfather," 69

gray a popular color for professional clothing, 56

grounded forced to stay on the ground, 17

grow into become, 88

guests the people one invites, 42

guest speaker someone invited to give a speech, 24

guys informal, slang for "people," 42

gym short for "gymnasium," 44

had to have insisted on owning, 20

half one of two equal parts, 55

hammock netting or material used for sleeping, which is hung between two trees or posts, 18

handsome good-looking, 26

happy cherry, merry, 22, 46, 49

hard bad, destructive, 48

hard cash coins, paper currency or money, 21

harsh cruel, hard, 32

have to must, 60

having fun enjoying yourself, 40

Hawaiian in Hawaii, 7

headquarters main office, 10

healthy in good physical condition, 88

heard listened to, 22

heaven's name, in an exclamation of surprise, 13

held up delayed; accosted and robbed, 24

help aid, assist, 88

highly very, extremely, 79

hint suggestion, 71

hold the line wait, 83

home-brewed made at home, 69

honest truthful, 63

honey affectionate form of address, 19

hour time of day or night, 43

how to what extent, 36

how about would you like, 55

how many what number (of people), 65

"how-to" book   a book with instructions on how to do something, 23

hydraulic lift   machine for raising heavy objects, 14

ideas   thoughts, 15

I'd say   I would estimate or guess, 26

ignore   do not pay attention to, 74

imagine   pretend, form a mental image, 35

in case   in the event that, 60

included   meant to have as part of something, 94

install   set up, put in place, 82

intensive   extremely dedicated, 36

interrupting   stopping for a moment, 55

in the doghouse   figurative for "in trouble," 85

invitation   request made to another person, 41

invite over   to ask to come to one's house, 41

iron, to   to remove wrinkles with an iron, to press, 51

ironing   the task of pressing clothes, 51

isn't about   does not deal with, 70

itch   irritation, tingling sensation, 87

jerky   dried beef, 81

job   piece of work, 45

jockeys   riders (on race horses), 78

jogging the memory   reminding someone, 49

jump, to   to leap in the air, 6

jury   twelve people who vote "guilty" or "not guilty" in a court of law, 56

just   only, 9, 80, 89; simply, 20, 35, 42, 60, 86; the instant, 81

just about   almost, 12

just here   in this exact spot, 58

kept up   did not allow to sleep, 69

kind   gentle, loving, 63

kind   type, 73

king   monarch, ruler, 96

know   are acquainted with, 3, 55

knowing his place   being aware of his position (within the company), 10

label   sign on a package, 88

largely   mostly, 96

last   final, 38

late   tardy, 63; dead, 24

laundry   clothing and other things to be washed, 31

leaf   growth on a tree, 3

leaving   going away, 89

lesson   class, period of instruction, 63

let's   "let us"; why don't we, 2, 66, 88

letters   written communications, 52

lifetime length of a person's life, 79

little not much, a bit, 4, 50; small, 25, 58, 71

look see, 48, 59; appear to be, 56, 80

looking for trying to find, 48

looks seems, appears, 33

lord and master title for the highest ruler, 96

lose be unable to use, 1

lost could not find, 86

lot of, a very many, 11

love extreme affection and caring, 52

luckily fortunately, 15

Ma'am short for "Madam," a form of polite address, 9

made it to arrived at, came to, 16

major important, 4

making a clean job of it doing something right, 34

marble hard, smooth stone, 80

married became husband and wife, 52

mean intend to say, 92

means of support source of the necessities of life, 25

meeting period of time set aside to discuss something, 17

meringue topping made with whipped egg whites, 64

mess untidy or cluttered condition, 2

metal substance such as iron, aluminum, etc., 31

mice plural of "mouse," 86

mind, on your thinking about, 53

minute ago, a a short time in the past, 58

miscalculation error, 94

mix package of ingredients, 68

mob, the a gang of criminals, 24

mom mother, 67

moment, at the now, this minute, 8

money currency, dollars, 14, 26, 84; wealth, fortune, 26

moody not happy, temperamental, 50

movable able to be moved, 29

move, to to change homes, 89

Mr. abbreviation for "Mister," 13, 18, 62

Ms. form of address for women (without reference to marital status), 6

need require, must have, 26, 46

neighborhood the area where one lives, 42

never at no time, 40

new recent, just started, 32, 73

next time on the following occasion, 57

nice good, well done, 45

now at this minute, 58, 59

no way not a good method, 99

of course   naturally, surely, 78

office supplies   items needed to work in an office, 79

officially   according to authorities, 96

old   not new; not young, 1, 3, 69

only   nothing but, 93

on time   at the correct hour, 16

open, don't   keep closed

opinion   what a person thinks about something, 46

optimist   person who considers only the good or positive, 46

order of business   item to be discussed, 5

out of   having no more of, 91

outsmarting   winning by being more clever, 66

out there   outside, 100

pajamas   clothing to wear while sleeping, 16

parents   mothers and fathers, 66

party   festive gathering of people, 16, 42

persuade, to   to convince, to talk into doing, 39

piano   musical instrument with black and white keys, 63

pie   a dessert made of crust and a filling, 8, 64

pizza   baked dough with tomato sauce, cheese and other toppings, 35

phone   short for "telephone," 12, 55

picked up   received, 33

pickle   vegetable, usually a cucumber, processed in vinegar, 72

pickle, in a   in trouble, 72

pinstripe   suit of material with evenly spaced narrow stripes, 56

plan   a proposed course of action, 17

playing rough   playing in a very physical or dangerous way, 19

pleasure   happy task, 98

plumber   person who works with or repairs water pipes, 62

popcorn   a snack made from corn kernels, 21

portable   able to be carried, 12

position   job, 96

possible   able to be done, 12

postal   of the mail, 52

pounding   hitting, 70

poverty   state of being poor, 52

pre-approved   approved in advance, 97

probably   likely to be, 24

problem   a situation that must be resolved, 5; difficulty, 27

promised   said that he or she would do something, 14

psychology   study of individual behavior, 66

pull yourself together   gain control of yourself, 17

punch, with a   with added zest, 73

puppy   young dog, 88

putting to the test   trying out, 56

quick fix   prepare fast, 68

quite   very, 1

race   competition of speed, 78

raise   an increase in salary, 14

raising hands   putting hands in the air (to vote), 5

read   seeing and understanding words on a page, 23

really   truly, in fact, 40, 100

receive, to   to be given, 97

referred to   called, 96

relax   calm yourself, 6, 93; rest, 95

remember   recall, do not forget, 28, 42

reminds   helps to remember, recall, 49

removed   took out, 69

rendition   performance, way of playing (on an instrument), 22

report, to   to announce; to inform someone of something, 37

runaway   fugitive, escaped, 37

sadder   more unhappy, 22

safety   for protection against injury, 82

sandwich   two slices of bread with filling (meat, cheese, etc.), 55

sarge   informal, short form of "sergeant," 32

saves   keeps for future use, 26, 30

scale   device for measuring weight, 63

score   total points, 98

screwdriver   a hand tool, 48

secret   hidden technique, 80

see   look, 88

seems   appears, 27

see-through   transparent; with a hole for looking through, 81

selected   chosen, 97

serious   grave, critical, 36

set up, to   to conduct, carry on, 12

shirt   item of clothing, 51

shivering   shaking from the cold, 85

shower   stall with spraying water for bathing, 34

signify   show, indicate, 5

sister's   sister's house, 35

sit   be seated, 74, 92

smart   intelligent, 63

smile   having a happy expression on your face, 40

smoke, to   to have a cigarette, 6

smoker   person who smokes cigarettes, 6

snow   precipitation in winter, 101

think, I   it seems to me, 4, 45, 91

think   have the opinion, 56

thinking about   considering, 62

thought   had the idea, 89

throw off, to   to remove by force, 70

ticket   fine issued by police for breaking a law or rule, 33

tie   item of men's clothing, 45

timer   device for measuring length of time, 71

today   on this day, 50

told   mentioned, 83

tonight   this evening, 2, 39, 41

too   very, 75

too much   a larger amount than necessary, 45

top, to the   to the head of the company, 11

toy   something to play with, 93

traffic   cars, trucks, etc., on a road, 24

tremendous   large in amount or number, 15

trying   attempting, 89

tried   made an attempt, 55

truly   really, truthfully, 68

turkey-helper   mixture for preparing turkey more quickly, 68

turned out   resulted in, 75

to turn in   to give to the authorities, 84

TV   short for "television," 47

tyranny   rule by a tyrant or dictator, 70

unanimous   agreed, all having the same opinion, 56

unexpected   not planned, not anticipated, 42

unhappy   not pleased, 50

unplug   pull out the electric plug or cord, 9

use   make use of, employ, 1, 31, 71, 72

vacation   period of rest and enjoyment, 7; trip, 89, 95

Vegas   Las Vegas (Nevada), 99

waiting   holding the line, 65

wakes up   rouses from sleep, 73

want   wish, desire, 51, 84

warm   sincere, friendly, 98

warned   told in advance, 3

warning   notice (before something happens), 1, 32

way, on my   on route to, 11

weak   not strong; feeble, 75

weight   amount (in pounds) a person weighs, 4

welcome   greeting, 98

well   an introductory word, 27, 51

wet   soaked in water, 100

wetsuit   protective clothing for divers, 100

while   during the time, 48

wife   married woman, 50, 74

wish   want, 37

without   with no, 1

wonder   ask oneself, 43

Points of Interest

The following notes help explain phrases and titles that appear throughout the book. Page numbers appear in heavy black type.

1   **losing your head**   When two young people fall in love, you can say they "lose their heads" over one another. This little expression explains those times when you temporarily lose control of yourself and do something that you do not usually do.

1   **use it or lose it**   Sometimes at work your employer may say about your vacation time: "Use it or lose it." In other words, if you do not use your vacation days, you will no longer have them for that year. The same idea can be applied to skills or even to a person's ability to think.

2   **eat out**   Eating out is a popular activity. Quite often, after a hard day's work, people will go to restaurants to eat rather than prepare dinner to eat at home.

3   **leaf blower**   People in the United States are fond of gadgets and devices that save them time or effort. An old-fashioned rake used to be good enough to put the leaves in a yard into a pile. Now, a noisy machine helps them to do the job with less physical effort.

3   **"Blowing in the Wind"**   This is the title of a popular song from the 1970s.

4   **breakthrough**   A major scientific or technical advance is called a breakthrough of knowledge. A cure for AIDS, for example, would be a medical breakthrough.

4   **gain weight**   One estimate states that more than 40 million people in the United States are overweight. Perhaps this accounts for the big business of diet foods and diet programs.

6   **smoker's last stand**   Custer's Last Stand refers to a famous event in U.S. history. General George Armstrong Custer led his men into battle against Native Americans and was promptly surrounded and defeated. People who smoke cigarettes are not in that position yet, but the places where they are allowed to smoke are being more and more limited every day.

7   write off   No one likes to pay taxes. One way to reduce the amount of taxes you pay is to write off, or deduct, an expense. The Internal Revenue Service (IRS) is the agency that is responsible for collecting taxes and making sure that people follow the rules and only write off expenses that are allowed.

8   pies   In Hollywood, the nation's movie-making center, throwing a pie in someone's face is an old tradition of comedy.

9   fax   Facsimile machines are one of many inventions that help people do business more quickly. *Fax* is a noun that stands for the machine and the piece of paper that contains a message that was received on the machine. It is also used as a verb to stand for the act of sending a message on the facsimile machine. In the spirit of free enterprise, many businesses are using the device to send advertisements to potential clients. On the one hand, the businesses are praised for their clever use of the fax machine. On the other hand, they are cursed by the people who do not want to receive "junk" messages.

9   Gimme the fax, ma'am.   Sergeant Joe Friday, a police officer on the television program "Dragnet," became famous for the line, "Just the facts, ma'am."

10   You are here.   Maps in big buildings or shopping centers usually are marked "You are here" to help people figure out how to reach their destination.

12   portable phone   Telephones are an important tool of business in the United States. Now, however, portable phones are everywhere—in cars, in restaurants, in movie theaters, and even on airplanes. Many people do not leave their homes without their portable phones.

15   bright ideas   Cartoonists draw a shining light bulb to represent a sudden idea or inspiration.

15   Research and Development   The Research and Development Department of a business is responsible for creating and testing new products.

16   on time   Punctuality is traditionally considered an important cultural value in the United States. In some companies, employees who are usually not punctual in arriving for work are penalized by having money subtracted from their paychecks.

16   pajama party   Pajama parties used to be popular with teenage girls. A group would stay overnight at one girl's house and have an informal party to listen to music, chat, tell stories, and so on.

17   pull yourself together   Staying in control of oneself and not doing anything ridiculous, damaging, or foolhardy is an important cultural value. One response to someone who has lost control is "Pull yourself together." More recently, the expression "Get a grip (on yourself)" has become a popular way to tell someone to regain control.

19   honey   In English there are many terms of endearment such as *honey, sweetheart, dear.* Usually, the terms are used affectionately between people who are very close. However, some people who are generally friendly and outgoing use the terms frequently, even with strangers.

19   spin the baby   "Spin the Bottle" used to be a popular game at parties. Players would take turns spinning a bottle. Whomever the bottle pointed to when it stopped spinning had to perform a stunt or do something silly. The game was often used as a way to give someone a kiss without being scolded.

20   for the birds   *For the birds* means "not worth anything" or "a very bad idea."

22   crying fowl / crying foul   "Crying foul" means to claim that an action taken by someone is unfair or illegal. In sports, it means claiming that a player has committed a foul, done something forbidden by the rules. "Crying fowl" means a weeping bird.

23   "how-to" books   People in the United States love to do things to improve their homes, their appearance, the way they raise children, etc. "How-to" books usually contain instructions on almost everything from how to fix a leaky faucet to how to be more handsome or more beautiful.

24   late   People use many expressions in English to avoid using the words *die* and *dead.* The "late entertainer," for example, refers to an entertainer who has died. Of course, *late* also refers to someone who has not arrived on time. The meaning is usually easily understood from the context of the conversation.

25 bring out the little boy in me A popular idea centers around mature adults still having their younger selves inside them. It probably stems from memories—that are not always accurate—of the happiness and spontaneity of being young.

27 dentist In popular magazines, lists are very common. Usually, "going to the dentist" appears in every list of "People's Worst Fears."

30 drive-in movies When going to drive-in movies was a popular activity, the movie theaters used to charge by the number of passengers in the car. Teenagers would attempt all sorts of tricks, such as hiding in the trunk of the car, to avoid paying for a ticket.

30 Trojan Horse According to legend, Greek soldiers build an enormous, hollow wooden horse and left it outside the gates of Troy. When the people of the city brought the horse inside the gates, the Greek soldiers jumped out and conquered the city.

32 drunk drivers Drunk drivers (people whose judgment and reactions have been weakened from the effects of alcoholic drinks on the mind and body) have become a major social issue in the United States. Drunk drivers have been responsible for many accidents and deaths on the highways. Even the beer companies have produced advertising to discourage people from driving if they have had too much to drink.

32 sobriety test One way police officers test drivers to determine whether they have had too much to drink is to ask them to walk a straight line.

33 no standing Signs marked "No stopping or standing" are often posted along busy streets. You cannot stop your car or wait even for a little while in a zone with this sign.

33 parking ticket A parking ticket is issued whenever someone has broken a rule of parking or has not put enough money in a parking meter. Usually, tickets are placed in the door handle, under the windshield wiper blade, or stuck to a window of the car.

35   pizza delivery   An alternative to dining in a restaurant is to order a pizza delivered to your home. Pizza is a favorite food in the United States, especially among young people.

37   getaway car   A band of robbers often appoints one person to stay outside the bank or store. This person's job is to wait in the car with the motor running so that the robbers can "get away" from the scene of the crime quickly.

38   cliffhanger   The old-time movies had serial thrillers called "cliffhangers." The movie was shown in weekly installments and usually ended with an exciting scene so that people would come back to the theater the following week. Often the hero or heroine was left hanging over the edge of a cliff or in some similarly dangerous situation.

38   last gas   Before the days of superhighways and fuel efficient cars, gas stations would have signs reading "Last Chance for Gas for 100 Miles," or whatever the distance was to the next town or gas station.

39   bowling night   People who have regular outings, such as bowling or playing cards with friends, will refer to the night of the activity as "my bowling night" or "my poker night" or "my bridge night."

40   Smile and the world smiles with you   A well-known saying is "Laugh and the world laughs with you. Cry and you cry alone." This is possibly a reflection of the cultural value of always appearing to be happy. It might also refer to the fickleness of your fellow human beings.

42   just drop by   A common invitation is "If you're ever in the neighborhood, just drop by." Quite often people give this casual invitation to friends and acquaintances. They rarely mean for the invitation to be taken seriously and they expect people to call them first before showing up at the doorstep.

44   gym equipment   People used to go to a gymnasium to exercise, but now they buy stationary bicycles, weightlifting machines, rowing machines, treadmills, and other pieces of equipment that permit them to exercise at home. Usually, the equipment is used during the first week or so and then it sits forever, gathering dust.

51 ironing board   Fold-down ironing boards used to be common in apartments and houses with very little space. Now, however, people can buy irons that will remove wrinkles while the clothing is still on the hanger.

54 onion-garlic sandwich   Home remedies and preventions have become popular once again, as more and more medicines are discovered to be harmful to the body. Both onion and garlic are said to be good for your health.

55 cordless phone   *See* **12** *portable phone.*

56 gray pinstripe   The pinstripe suit has become the symbol of the serious, conservative man. In recent years, clothing has been "analyzed" and used to create a specific image for success in a person's endeavors.

57 case the joint   *Case the joint* is slang originally used by gangsters. A burglar who cases a joint first has studied the layout of the place to be robbed and has made note of the usual comings and goings of the people.

58 carried away   Being or "getting" carried away means you become so involved or engrossed in something that you lose sight of your surroundings, the rules of etiquette, etc. It can also refer to someone who is too enthusiastic about something.

59 Don't look now.   This expression indicates that the speaker really *wants* you to look, but the time is not right. An example might be: "Don't look now, but isn't that your married neighbor who is kissing that stranger?"

61 Thanks, anyway   This expression is a polite form of refusal when people are kind enough to offer you something you are embarrassed to refuse.

62 girl plumber   Times have changed and now girls grow up to be plumbers, carpenters, and electricians. In fact, they qualify for all sorts of other jobs that used to be filled only by men.

66 child psychology   Books that offer advice on how to raise children are very popular in the United States.

68   Thanksgiving   Thanksgiving is a national holiday of the United States. It is celebrated on the fourth Thursday of every November to commemorate the help given to the Pilgrims by the Native Americans. In modern times, the day is celebrated with family gatherings and a traditional meal of turkey, stuffing, cranberry sauce, pumpkin pie, and other dishes.

68   turkey-helper   Although many people in the United States prefer to cook the old-fashioned way, many others use the mixes and other prepared foods available in supermarkets to shorten the time spent in the kitchen.

68   working mother   In many families in the United States, both parents have jobs outside the home. *Working mother* refers to the fact that the mother has a job.

69   caffeine   Caffeine has been the subject of many scientific studies in the United States. Most of them conclude that caffeine is harmful to the human body. Caffeine is also said to interfere with sleep because it is a stimulant. Almost all the coffee companies offer decaffeinated coffee, which is coffee from which the caffeine has been removed.

71   "Smoke Gets in Your Eyes"   This is the title of a popular romantic song about how love can blind a person.

71   smoke alarm   Smoke alarms are among the many safety devices that have been made available in recent years. The device contains a sensor that can detect smoke. When smoke is detected, an alarm sounds.

73   decaf   Short for "decaffeinated coffee." *(See also* **69** *caffeine.)*

74   breakfast table   Reading the newspaper while eating breakfast is a favorite custom in the United States.

75   diet   Dieting has become an obsession in the United States, especially diet plans that claim to help people lose weight quickly. In recent years, businesses have been established to help people lose weight. *See also* **4** *gain weight.*

76   more coffee   People in the United States drink great quantities of coffee. Most restaurants charge for a cup of coffee and offer as many refills of the cup as the person likes. *(See also* **69** *caffeine;* **73** *decaf.)*

77   hot dogs   Hot dogs have been a favorite food in the United States for many years. In large cities, vendors often sell hot dogs on the street corners. Hot dogs are also popular at ball games, fairs, and other outdoor gatherings.

80   I don't know much about art, but . . .   This is short for "I don't know much about art, but I know what I like," a popular expression meaning that the person has not formally studied art but has his or her own tastes.

81   jerky   Jerky is hard, dried beef, usually available in the form of a stick. Historically, soldiers (such as those during the Civil War) carried jerky because it would not spoil and could be carried easily. Today, campers and hikers use it for the same reason.

82   Along came a spider   A line from a children's rhyme: "Little Miss Muffet / sat on a tuffet, / eating her curds and whey. / Along came a spider / who sat down beside her, / and frightened Miss Muffet away."

83   hold the line   This is another way of telling a person not to hang up the phone.

84   Federal Bureau of Investigation   A government agency that handles enforcement of federal laws. It is usually referred to as the FBI.

84 $16 bill   Paper currency in the United States is issued in one-, five-, ten-, twenty-, fifty-, and one-hundred-dollar bills. Some two-dollar bills exist, but they are not commonly printed by the U.S. Treasury.

86   When the cat's away   The complete expression is "When the cat's away, the mice will play."

87   starting from scratch   This expression means "beginning with the basic ingredients" and is used figuratively to mean "starting again after something has failed or gone wrong."

91   dog-tired   When people feel extremely tired, they sometimes say they are "dog-tired."

92   dog's chair   People in the United States often treat their pets as though they were members of the family. Pets often are allowed to sit or sleep on the furniture and move about the house freely.

93 **house-broken** Pets are usually trained to eliminate outside the house. When a pet has learned to indicate to its owner that it wants to be let outside, it is said to be house-broken.

94 **Noah** According to the Bible, God instructed Noah to build an ark (a ship) and to take two of every species aboard to save the animals from the flooding rains that would last forty days and forty nights.

95 **take a cruise** Taking a cruise, or a trip on an oceanliner, is a popular form of vacation for those people who can afford it.

97 **credit** Credit and credit cards are popular forms of payment in the United States. Most companies have access to a person's credit history, which is a record of how well the individual has paid the monthly bill.

98 **basketball team** Basketball teams not only compete during games but also compete to find the tallest players who can most easily toss the ball into the ten-foot-high basket.

98 **Lilliput** *Gulliver's Travels* is a famous novel by Jonathan Swift. Gulliver is shipwrecked and washed ashore on the land of Lilliput, a kingdom of tiny people.

99 **baggage claim** The baggage claim is the area in the airport where passengers pick up their luggage after a flight.

99 **Las Vegas** Las Vegas, Nevada, is famous for its legal gambling casinos and nightclubs.

101 **Gone with the snow** *Gone with the Wind* is the title of a famous novel by Margaret Mitchell about a romance during the Civil War.